welcome to the *world*

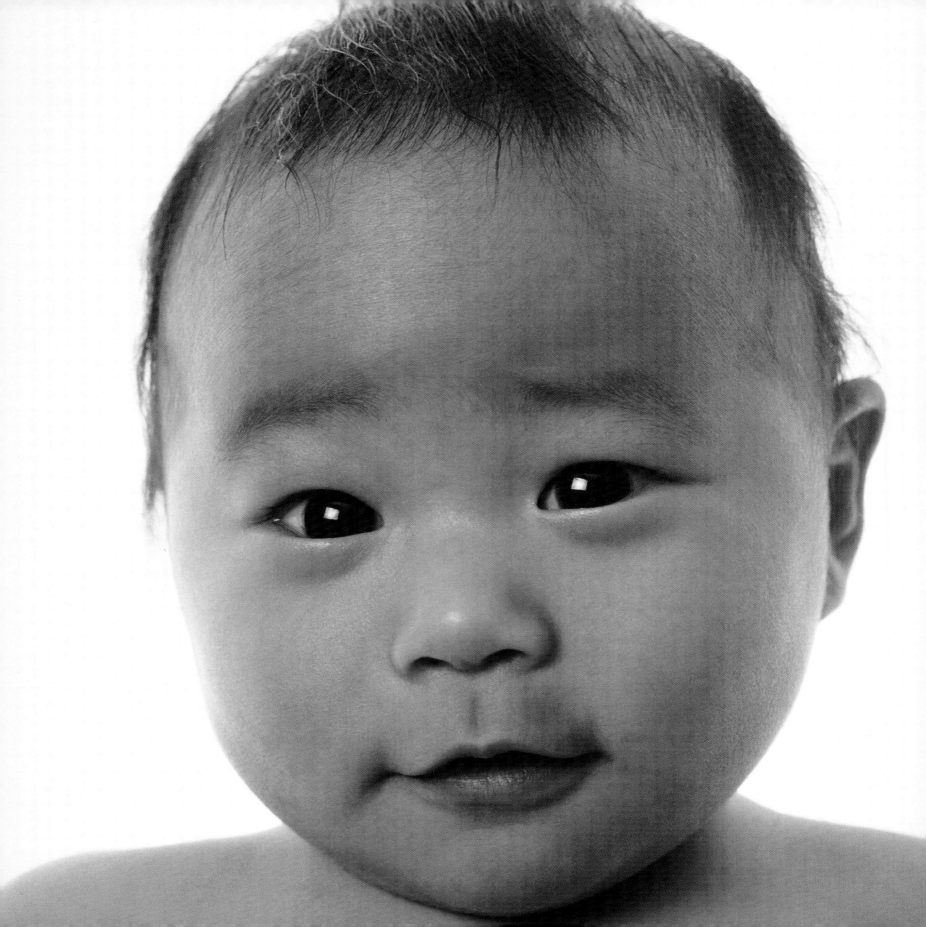

welcome to the
world

A Celebration of Birth and Babies from Many Cultures

Compiled by Nikki Siegen-Smith

Barefoot Books
Celebrating Art and Story

Contents

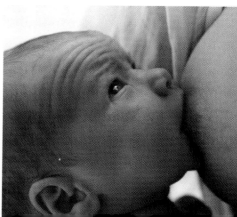

The Conceiving

Now

you are in the ark of my blood

in the river of my bones

in the woodland of my muscles

in the ligaments of my hair

in the wit of my hands

in the smear of my shadow

in the armada of my brain

under the stars of my skull

in the arms of my womb

Now you are here

you worker in the gold of flesh

Penelope Shuttle
England

To Our Daughter

And she is beautiful, our daughter.
Only six months, but a person.
She turns to look at everything, out walking.
All so precious. I mustn't disturb it with words.
People are like great clowns,
Blossom like balloons, black pigeons like eagles,
Water beyond belief.

She holds out her hand to air,
Sea, sky, wind, sun, movement, stillness,
And wants to hold them all.
My finger is her earth connection, me, and earth.

Her head is like an apple, or an egg.
Skin stretched fine over a strong casing,
Her whole being developing from within
And from without: the answer.

And she sings, long notes from the belly or the throat,
Her legs kick her feet up to her nose,
She rests – laid still like a large rose.

She is our child,
The world is not hers, she has to win it.

Jennifer Armitage
Western Europe

Moonbelly

Drumseed
        a-bloom
wit de speed
        of water

daddywater
        meet
mammywater
        in one twinkling

monthly blood
turn back
it own tide

monthly blood
have new mouth
to feed

an new mouth is new bud

When mammywater
an daddywater
meet

Wit good blessing
spirits willing

        navel string
           soon sing

John Agard
Caribbean

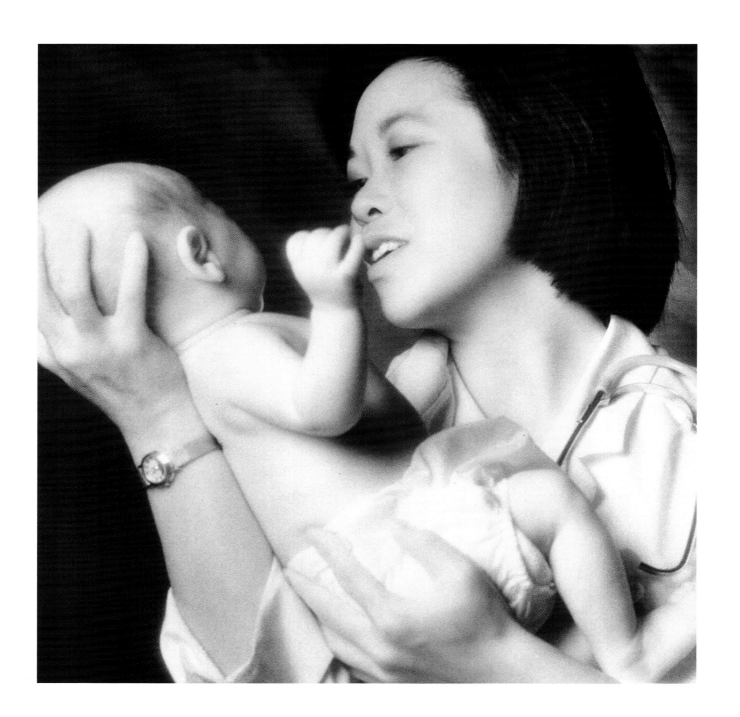

Birth

My thought was gradually stilled
Around this unseen life,
Turning in silent fluid,
Unborn to air or light.
My hands, external and crude,
Feel for the beating heart,
The head, the buttocks, a knee;
But I cannot properly know,
I cannot see.

"The pain is to open the way,"
My old servant told me.
"The pain is to open the door
Of that dark corridor to life."

"Nur Hayati anak siapa?
Nur Hayati anak Rosmawati."

"Nur Hayati, whose child?
Nur Hayati, the child of Rosmawati."

So very small is she,
Her face seems still half-closed.
"Like buds they are, eh Cik Rose?
Slowly they unfold,
Like buds they unfold."

Little bud, her hair smells of feathers.
Her grandfather's hair is white,
And his face, it brims with light.
The bud that has yet to unfold,
The body that gives up its hold.

Rosemary Mokhtar
Southeast Asia

On the First Night

On the first night
of the full moon,
the primeval sack of ocean
broke,
& I gave birth to you
little woman,
little carrot top,
little turned-up nose,
pushing you out of myself
as my mother
pushed
me out of herself,
as her mother did,
& her mother's mother before her,
all of us born
of woman.

I am the second daughter
of a second daughter
of a second daughter,
but you shall be the first.
You shall see the phrase
"the second sex"
only in puzzlement,
wondering how anyone,

except a madman,
could call you "second"
when you are so splendidly
first,
conferring even on your mother
firstness, vastness, fullness
as the moon at its fullest
lights up the sky.
Now the moon is full again
& you are four weeks old.
Little lion, lioness,
yowling for my breasts,
growling at the moon,
your red face demanding,
your hungry mouth howling,
your screams, your cries
which all spell life
in large letters
the color of blood.

You are born a woman
for the sheer glory of it,
little redhead, beautiful screamer.
You are no second sex,
but the first of the first;

& when the moon's phases
fill out the cycle
of your life,
you will crow
for the joy
of being a woman,
telling the pallid moon
to go drown herself
in the blue ocean,
& glorying, glorying, glorying
in the rosy wonder
of your sunshining wondrous
self.

Erica Jong
USA

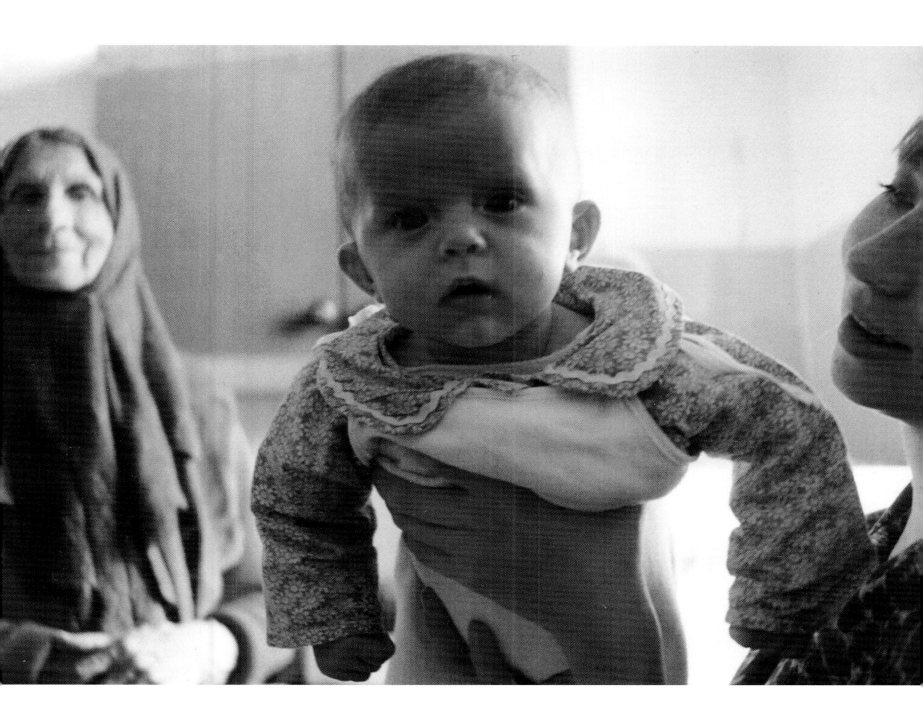

What Is My Name?

You may not call me beautiful or
       the spirits will steal me away,
       especially if I'm fat.

I have no name till my family see
       if I'm happy, hungry or cross,
       then call me that!

Anonymous
Cambodia

Dawn

Of your hand I could say this
a bird poised mid-air in flight
as delicate and smooth.

Of your mouth
a foxglove in its taking
without edges or hurt.

This of your ear
a tiny sea-horse, immortal
sporting in white waves

and of your eye
a place where no one could hide
nothing lurk.

Of your cupped flesh
smooth in my palm
an agate on the sea-shore.

Of your back and belly
that they command kisses.
And of your feet I would say

they are inquisitive and gay
as squirrels or birds
and so return to your hand

and begin my voyage
around your loveliness
again and yet again

as in my arms you lie sleeping.

Jeni Couzyn
South Africa

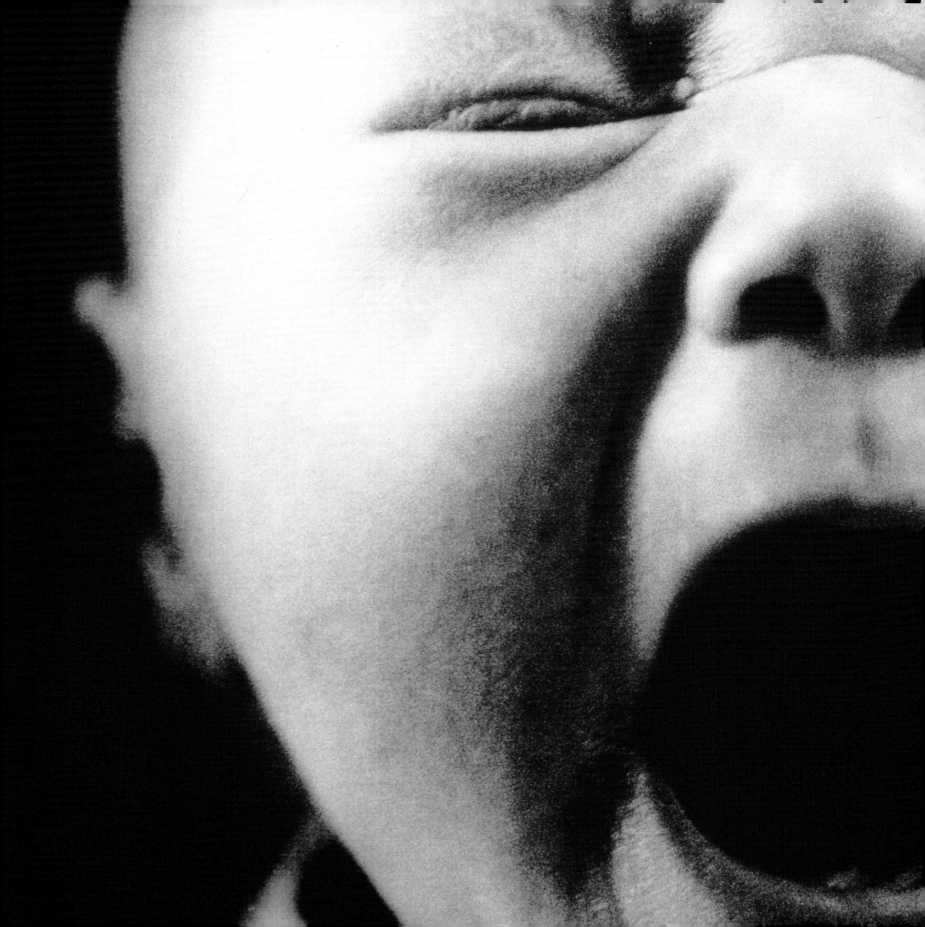

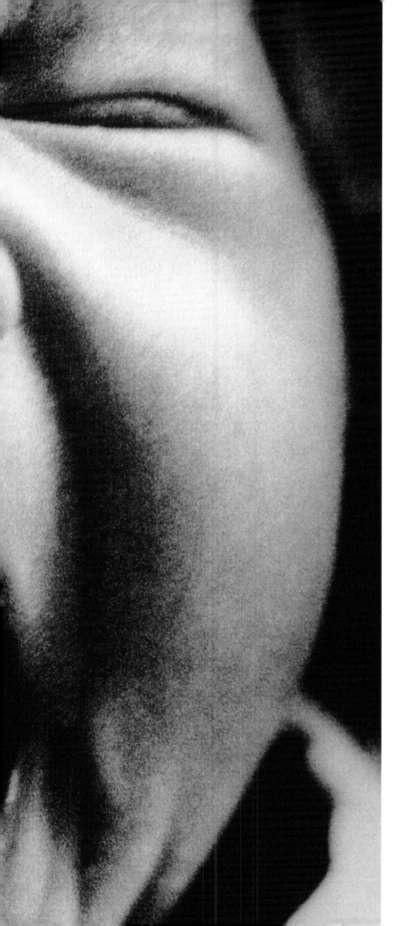

Morning Song

Love set you going like a fat gold watch.
The midwife slapped your footsoles, and your bald cry
Took its place among the elements.

Our voices echo, magnifying your arrival. New statue.
In a drafty museum, your nakedness
Shadows our safety. We stand round blankly as walls.

I'm no more your mother
Than the cloud that distils a mirror to reflect its own slow
Effacement at the wind's hand.

All night your moth-breath
Flickers among the flat pink roses. I wake to listen:
A far sea moves in my ear.

One cry, and I stumble from bed, cow-heavy and floral
In my Victorian nightgown.
Your mouth opens clean as a cat's. The window square

Whitens and swallows its dull stars. And now you try
Your handful of notes;
The clear vowels rise like balloons.

Sylvia Plath
USA

Mother's Song
to a Baby

First
this little baby
has been given life
through the medicine man's song
through the medicine man's prayer
for this baby the songs
have been sung

Next
the baby's mother
has taken care of him
with the songs of the rain gods

This
little baby
in his cloud-cradle
was watched over
by his mother

It
was
nice
how the clouds
came up like foam
and
as if he
was among them
this little baby
was cared for

Anonymous, Inuit, USA

A Poem for My Son

I seem to know all about you:
your time, your place, your name,
the clean Indian-wheat colour of your skin,
your unpolished words.
But I know that there are also sounds
that you do not know, shapes
that you wouldn't recognise.
For instance, the owl's lean cry,
or the sea at Puri
during a small moon's night.
And, at this hour, when
you are breathing so quietly
beside your mother,
I seem to hear a remote whisper
that almost tells me
that you are not mine.
I hear the owl's cry,
the gentle, expanding roar of
the blue waters of Puri,
But I know where my night presently sleeps,
undisturbed by every thought,
so peacefully.

Bibhu Padhi
India

Praise of a Child

A child is like a rare bird.
A child is precious like coral.
A child is precious like brass.
You cannot buy a child on the market.
Not for all the money in the world.
The child you can buy for money is a slave.
We may have twenty slaves,
We may have thirty labourers,
Only a child brings us joy,
One's child is one's child.
The buttocks of our child are not so flat
That we should tie the beads on another child's hips.
One's child is one's child.
It may have a watery head or a square head,
One's child is one's child.
It is better to leave behind a child,
Than let the slaves inherit one's house.
One must not rejoice too soon over a child.
Only the one who is buried by his child,
Is the one who has truly borne a child.
On the day of our death, our hand cannot hold a single cowrie.
We need a child to inherit our belongings.

Anonymous
Yoruba, Africa

Lullaby

O my son, born on a winter's morn,
The way is long and you are alone,
Your ancestors watch you from afar,
Will you be the next bright star?
O my son, born into war,
Grow swiftly, that you might wear
Their mantle, if you dare.
Greet them without fear,
You will be remembered there.
Kaka feather on your spear,
Feather of an albatross in your hair –
Land, sea and air
Here in the hollow of my hand –
Take them, lest they disappear.

Anonymous
Maori, New Zealand

Sonne

Could
anything
mean more to me
right now
than the
boy's smile
as he turns
on belly
lifting his face –

his
muscles
get
stronger

he laughs
throwing his
head back
as I toss him
around my lap

and he wants
to put the purple iris
inside
his pink mouth

no no
no no no, nothing.

Anne Waldman
USA

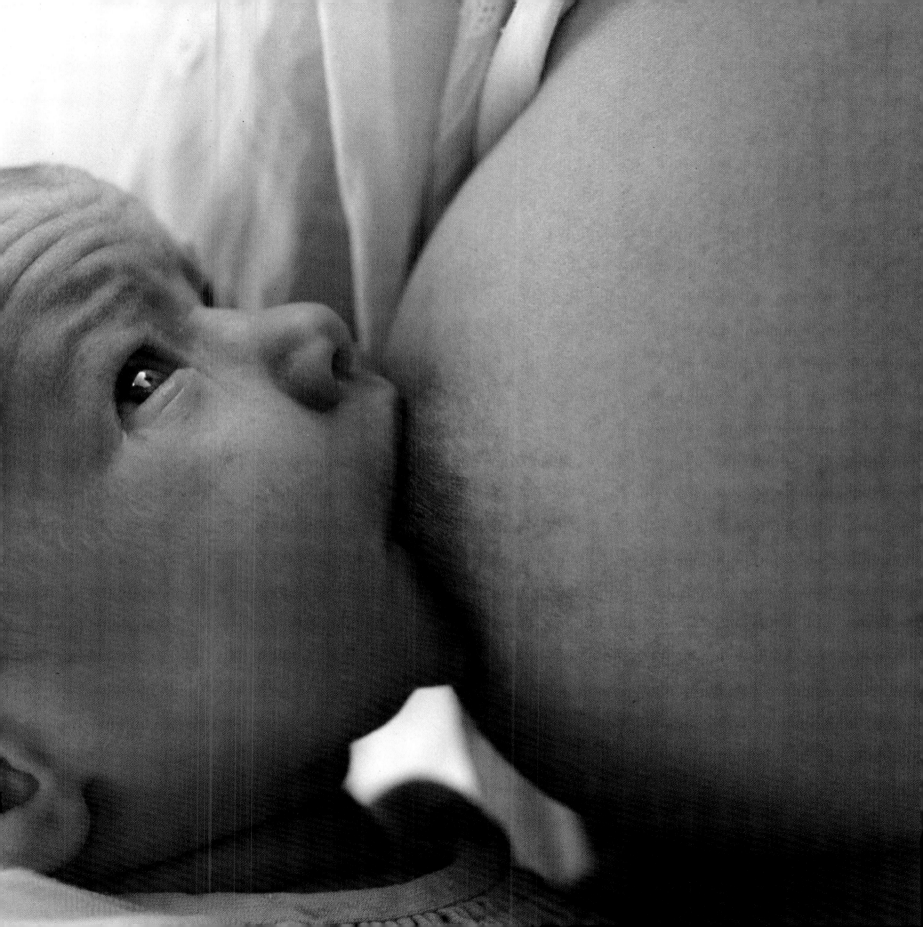

The Washing of the Infant

Most men, bringing up sons, wish for them intellect;

But I by my intellect have had a life-time of failure.

I would only desire that my child should be simple and dull,

That with no ill-fortune and no troubles he may attain to highest office.

Su Shih
China

Haiku

having put to sleep
the child there's the laundry now
and the summer moon

Issa
Japan

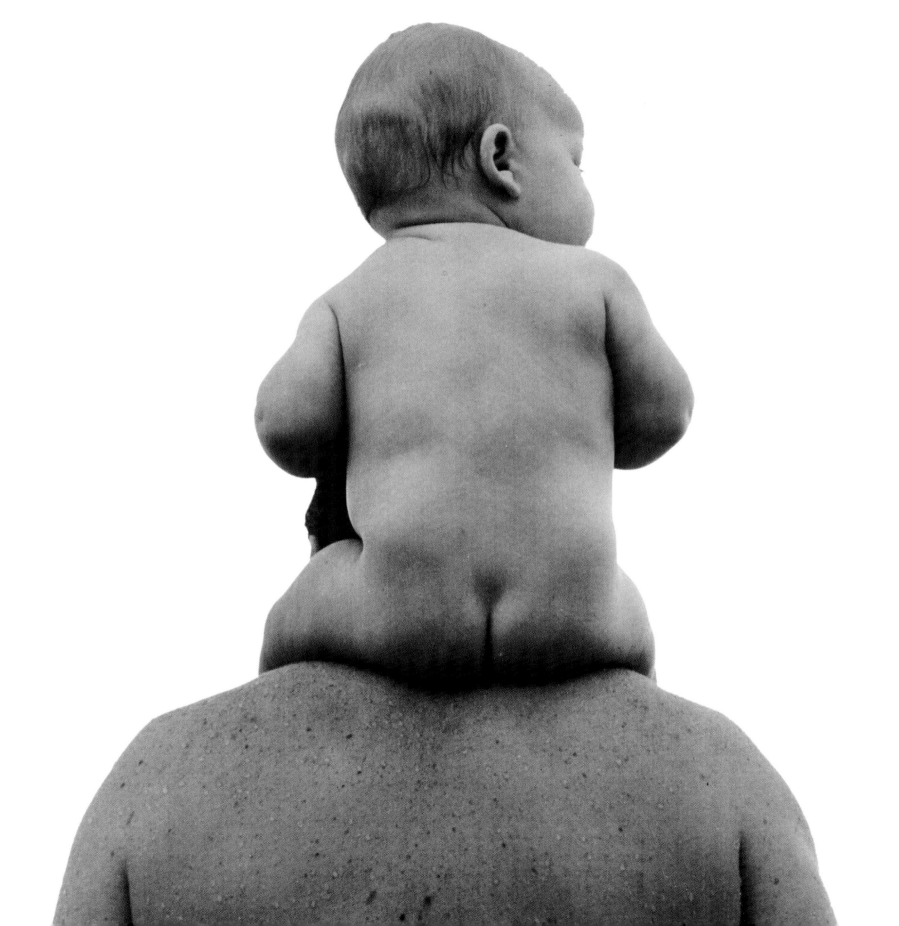

I Will Show You Beauty

Come, my son,
    to see the reasons why you were conceived
    to know why you happened.
    I will show you the beauty of the breath breathed
into you,
    I will show you the world
    that is a richness of acres between your feet.

Come, my son,
    I will show you the sheep
    that keep the Gwryd tidy with their kisses,
    the cow and her calf in Cefri Llan,
    foxgloves and bluebells
    and honeysuckle on a hedgerow in Rhyd-y-fro;

    I will show you how to fashion
    a whistle from the twigs of the great sycamore-tree
    in the incomparable woods of John Bifan,
    how to look for nests on the slopes of Bari Bach,
    how to swim naked in the river;

    I will show you the thick undergrowth
    between Ifan's farm and the grey Vicarage,
    where the blackberries are legion
    and the chestnuts still on the floor;

    I will show you the bilberries thick
    on the scattered clumps of mountain moss;

    I will show you the toad
    in the damp dusk,
    and the old workings beneath the growing hay;

    I will show you the house where Gwenalt was born.

Come, my son,
    in your father's hand,
    and I will show you the beauty
    that lives in your mother's blue eyes.

Dafydd Rowlands
Wales

Baby Where Has Your Father Gone?

Baby where has your father gone?

Father went to steal banana seedlings.

Baby where has your mother gone?

Mother went to steal taro plants.

Your father is caught by banana roots –

Your mother is caught by taro roots –

When your mother arrives, you will feed hungrily.

Momoro Kini
Papua New Guinea

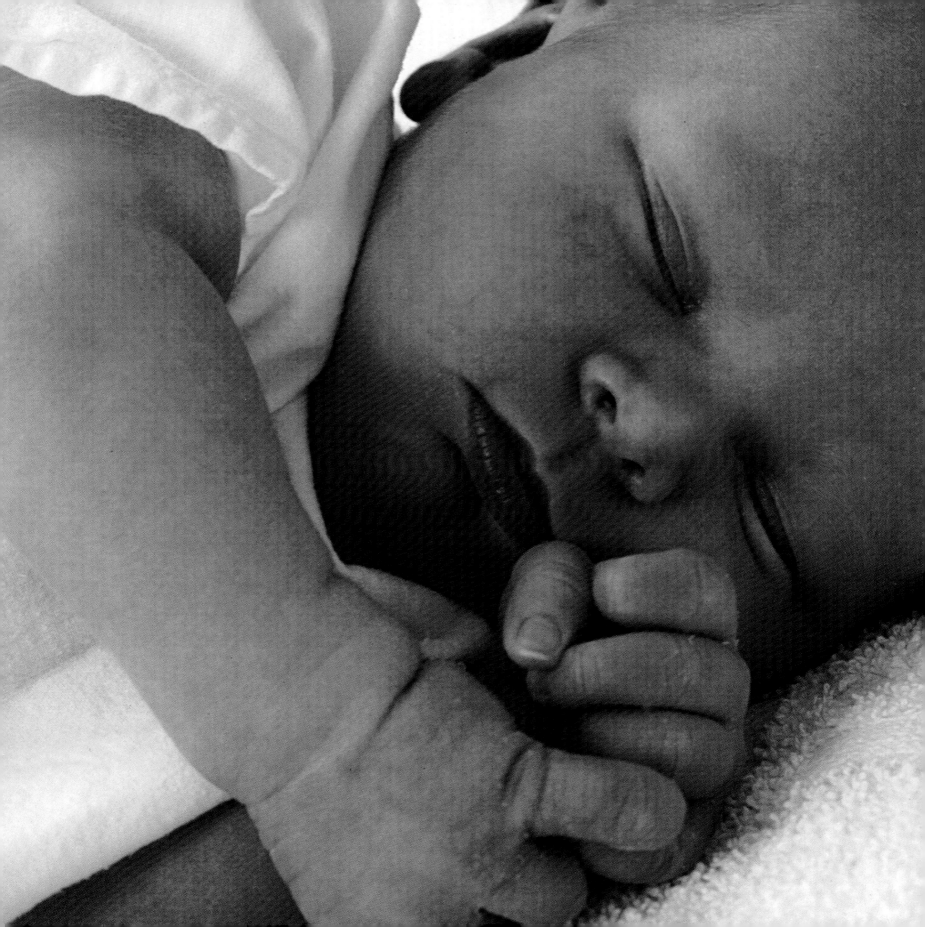

Night Feed

This is dawn.
Believe me
This is your season, little daughter.
The moment daisies open,
The hour mercurial rainwater
Makes a mirror for sparrows.
It's time we drowned our sorrows.

I tiptoe in.
I lift you up
Wriggling
In your rosy, zipped sleeper.
Yes, this is the hour
For the early bird and me
When finder is keeper.

I crook the bottle.
How you suckle!
This is the best I can be,
Housewife
To this nursery
Where you hold on,
Dear life.

A silt of milk
The last suck.
And now your eyes are open,
Birth-coloured and offended.
Earth wakes.
You go back to sleep.
The feed is ended.

Worms turn
Stars go in.
Even the moon is losing face.
Poplars stilt for dawn
And we begin
The long fall from grace.
I tuck you in.

And though your absence
fills my house
I give you back the sun and the wide night now
my precious one.

Eavan Boland
Ireland

Baby Running Barefoot

When the white feet of the baby beat across the grass
The little white feet nod like white flowers in a wind,
They poise and run like puffs of wind that pass
Over water where the weeds are thinned.

And the sight of their white playing in the grass
Is winsome as a robin's song, so fluttering;
Or like two butterflies that settle on a glass
Cup for a moment, soft little wing-beats uttering.

And I wish that the baby would tack across here to me
Like a wind-shadow running on a pond, so she could stand
With two little bare white feet upon my knee
And I could feel her feet in either hand

Cool as syringa buds in morning hours,
Or firm and silken as young peony flowers.

D. H. Lawrence
England

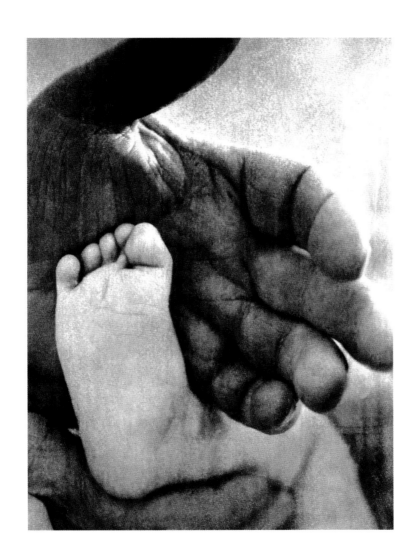

Children with Candles

The children are the candles white,
Their voices are the flickering light.

The children are the candles pale,
Their sweet song wavers in the gale.

Storm, abate! Wind, turn about!
Or you will blow their voices out.

Gerda Mayer
The Czech Republic

Birthing Traditions

All cultures have ways, new and old, of welcoming babies to the world. The traditions signify the way each culture prepares the baby for its new life. Rituals and ceremonies vary from culture to culture, but their elements are often similar. Newborn babies are cleansed, freed from enchantment, protected from evil and initiated into the community. In some cultures, they are named soon after birth; in others, a name is given in early childhood to reflect a particular trait in the child's personality.

An ancient Anglo-Saxon tradition was for women to pass sick babies through an ash tree. The stem of an ash sapling was cut in two and the naked child passed through it three times. After the ceremony, the tree was bound together and rubbed with soil. It was believed that, if the split healed, the child and tree would continue to grow healthily.

In southern Africa, when a Shona baby is born gifts of flour are brought. After the umbilical cord is cut, the midwife washes the child in warm water and herbal medicines made from plant roots. The child is bathed in this way over a period of several days – the plant roots are kept in a calabash filled with water and replaced when they get stale. To prevent the baby getting diarrhoea, the mother takes a little herbal medicine in her mouth and transfers it to the infant's mouth. A talisman, usually made from a sheep's skull, is tied around the baby's neck to protect it from diseases of the head, and a small ceremonial axe is bound to the back of the child's neck to keep it straight. Because it is thought that evil may enter through the fontanelle, another preparation made from plant roots is given to the child or, if the child becomes sick, is mixed with castor oil and rubbed on the fontanelle.

In past centuries, an Irish mother who wished her newborn son to die fighting would place the child's first food on her husband's sword and carefully feed it to the boy.

A Hindu father puts his mouth to the right ear of a newborn baby and whispers 'speak' three times. He then gives the child a name and feeds the baby with clotted milk, honey and butter from a vessel of pure gold.

It is traditional among the Inuit living in the Arctic circle for the mother to cut her baby's umbilical cord with a sharp stone which she will then keep in her clothes bag all her life. When she has given birth, members of the family tie a cord tightly around the mother's hips to bring her bones back into place. The placenta is put in a corner of the tent, or out in the open, and a miniature tent placed over it. Later, a blood-painting ceremony is held. The family slaughter a reindeer and paint blood on the faces of the mother, the child and other members of the family. The mother holds a stone, or piece of her or the child's clothing, suspended over the child and recites the names of all their ancestors. When the 'divining' stone or piece of clothing moves, the name the mother has just recited is given to the child. While the child is still small, a shaman or wise person ties pictures of the child's parents to its clothes, and the child and parents are given necklaces of red stone bound in leather. The shaman then chants: 'You are not on this earth; you are within this stone. No wind may reach you; no iceberg may crush you, but it will break in pieces against the edges of this stone.' The Inuit believe that, if a child is born prematurely, the mother should wrap the baby in the soft skin of a seabird and hang it over a small oil lamp for up to four weeks. She should feed the baby with oil and expressed breast milk until the baby can suckle for itself.

In Cairo, a seven-day naming ceremony is traditionally held, in which the midwife shakes the newborn in a sieve while telling it to obey its parents. The mother gives dried nuts, a symbol of fertility, to those bringing greetings to the new baby.

In rural parts of Malaysia, when a baby is born the umbilical cord is cut and the end wrapped with thread. The baby's father puts a paste made from leaves with magical properties on the child's big toe and makes a cross on its forehead and stomach. One of the child's grandmothers bathes it and wraps it in a soft cloth. After forty-four days, the placenta, which has been preserved in salt, turmeric root and pieces of asam gelugor (a type of fruit), is buried by the child's father underneath a coconut-palm seedling. Sometimes the umbilical cord is buried with the placenta or sometimes it is kept for its medicinal properties.

The mother or grandmother of a newborn Zulu infant feeds the child a watery porridge or the milk of a cow that has just given birth. The mother expresses her colostrum and does not begin breastfeeding until a day or two after the birth. The mother

and grandmother make a fire of herbs and pass the infant through the smoke, then rub red soil or ash on the baby's umbilical cord. In secret, the women hide the placenta, cord and childbirth blood, in the belief that, should these fall into the hands of an ill-wishing woman, they could provide a potent source of evil magic.

Traditionally, an Akha mother from South-east Asia eats a meal of rice to purify herself after giving birth. When her child is thirteen days old, she walks with the infant out of the village to the fields. Then, taking some cooked rice wrapped in a banana leaf, she rubs a little on to the child's lips. This is its first rice meal.

According to Aryan tradition, nurses took newborn infants and passed them through holes in stones, gaps in brambles and 'elfin' holes in trees in order to remove enchantment from the child. An ancient text states: 'If a child will not learn to go alone, let it creep silently, on three Friday mornings, through the bough of a bramble, both ends of which are growing in the earth.'

In the Himalayas, at the rising of the morning star – signifying newness, wisdom and learning – the grandmother of a Pon baby collects water and brings it to the mother and infant. The family give the baby a turquoise stone, representing the child's family mountain, its family tree and its family lake. When the umbilical cord is cut, it is thought that the *la*, consciousness and life, of the child comes into being. As butter and milk signify divinity and purity to the Pon, an image of a sheep is made from butter and the child is washed in milk.

In India, a traditional cleansing ceremony is held for Santal babies. A barber cuts a small patch of hair on the baby's head. He then collects the cut hair in a cup made from a leaf, pours oil on it and hands it to the midwife. Mixing oil with earth and turmeric, she rubs it on the bare scalp of the child. The Santal men then go away to wash. Using two strands of cotton, the midwife wraps up the arrow that cut the umbilical cord, takes the cut hair and goes to bathe with the other Santal women. At the water tank, she plants the arrow in the water, paints black and vermilion marks on the ground and lets one cotton thread and the hair float away in the water. She soaks the other thread in turmeric and ties it around the child's waist.

According to custom, the Yakut of Siberia believe that in the days before childbirth the mother should not eat swan or the eggs of wild birds, or else the child might be born deaf or handicapped. The Yakut call upon the goddess Ayisit to help the mother. When the baby is born, the family melt fat, which they then eat. The old woman who has attended the birth spills some fat into the fire and thanks Ayisit. For three days, no man may come into the *yurta*, or tent, of the newly born child. After three days, the old woman takes the placenta, along with straw from the bed, and places it high up in a tree.

Using the ashes from an extinct volcano, the Hopi of North America would rub the newborn baby's skin to clean it and make it soft.

The Chuvash live on the banks of the Volga River in the former Soviet Union. They have always held men and women in equal esteem. According to tradition, the parents would carve the umbilical cord of a newborn baby on the handle of a tool – for a boy, a tool used by his father and, for a girl, an implement used by her mother. In the case of a boy, the father would then say: 'Be like your father – a master of all trades.' In the case of a girl, the mother would say: 'Be hardworking like your mother – a skilful worker.'

Traditionally, a variety of cultures – European mothers until two hundred years ago, the Inuit and the Chagga people from East Africa – lick their babies clean at birth.

The Bang Chan people of Thailand would lay the baby on a winnowing tray along with the bamboo knife used to cut the cord, the soil that soothed the mother's vagina as the baby was born and things that represent the parents' hopes for the baby, such as a book for knowledge or a needle for intelligence.

When a child is born in Ladakh, northern India, it is traditional for the mother and baby to stay quietly in a separate room of the house. The family bring the mother and baby rich milk and yak butter and hang an arrow of good fortune from the willow roof. On the seventh day, friends bring flour, butter and little dough figures in the shape of an ibex – the horse of the gods. Monks burn incense and chant protective mantras. A month after the birth, the blacksmith comes with a spoon and a bracelet. When the child goes out for the first time, the parents rub its head with butter for good luck, paint a black mark of oil and soot on the forehead to warn off evil spirits and dress it in a woven robe, placing on its woollen hat an *om* crafted in silver.

ceremony

Sources

The Photographs

Phil Borges, Tony Stone Images: for nurse holding baby (p. 12). **Penny Gentieu, Tony Stone Images:** for Asian baby (frontispiece; p. 16). **Noel Griggs, Royal Photographic Society:** for 'babyhood' (p. 35). **Julia Ling, Royal Photographic Society:** for baby in *ba'* (Contents; p. 32). **Sally Mayman, Tony Stone Images:** for man carrying baby (p. 36; back cover). **Genna Naccache, Telegraph Colour Library:** for baby looking under towel (pp. 38-9). **Gopinder Kaur Panesar:** for grandmother and mother with baby (p. 15). **Steve McCurry, Magnum Photos:** for woman carrying her child through Barkhor, the last traditional Tibetan quarter of Lhasa (pp. 8-9). **Reflections Photolibrary, Bath:** for pregnant woman (p. 7); mother in profile (front cover; Contents; pp. 10-11); African woman hoeing (pp. 22-3); baby sleeping (p. 24); Chinese father and child (p. 28); breastfeeding baby (Contents; pp. 30-1); newborn sleeping (p. 40). **Carlos Reyes-Manzo, Andes Press Agency:** for grandmother and baby (Contents; pp. 26-7); Bosnian mother and child (pp. 44-5). **Rod Shone, Telegraph Colour Library:** for baby screaming (pp. 20-1). **Telegraph Colour Library:** for foot in hand (p. 43). **Baldev Singh Thethy:** for mother and child lying on pillow (p. 19).

The Poems

Grateful acknowledgment is made to the following for permission to print the material listed below.

Sue J. Batchelor: for 'What Is My Name?' Reprinted by kind permission. **Carcanet Press Ltd:** for 'Night Feed' from *Night Feed* by Eavan Boland. Copyright © 1995 by Carcanet Press. **Gomer Press:** for 'I Will Show You Beauty' by Dafydd Rowlands, from *Poetry from Wales 1930-1970*, ed. R. Gerallt Jones. Copyright © 1974 by Gomer Press. **Gerda Mayer:** for 'Children with Candles' from *Time Watching*, published by Hearing Eye, 1995. First published in *Ambit*, 1990. Copyright © by Gerda Mayer. Reprinted by permission of the author. **Oxford University Press:** for 'The Conceiving' from *The Orchard Upstairs* by Penelope Shuttle. Copyright © 1980 by Penelope Shuttle. **Laurence Pollinger Ltd and the Estate of Freida Lawrence Ravagli:** for 'Baby Running Barefoot' by D. H. Lawrence. First published in *English Review*, November 1909, and by Duckworth in *Amores*, 1916. **Serpent's Tail:** for an excerpt from 'Moonbelly' from *Mangoes and Bullets* by John Agard. Copyright ©1985 by John Agard. Reprinted by permission of Serpent's Tail.

Other material included in this collection has been taken from the following sources:

Bloodaxe Books Ltd: 'Dawn' from *Life by Drowning* by Jeni Couzyn, 1985. **Faber & Faber Ltd:** 'Morning Song' from *Ariel* by Sylvia Plath, 1965. **Gnomon Press:** 'Haiku' by Issa, from *Little Enough; 49 Haiki* by Basho et al., adapted by Cid Corman, 1991. **Heinemann Educational (Asia):** 'Birth' by Rosemary Mokhtar, from *Westerly* (Southeast Asian Issue), No. 4, December 1976. **Iris:** 'Sonne' by Anne Waldman, from *First Baby Poems*, 1977. **Mabari Publications:** 'Praise of a Child' from *The Moon Cannot Fight*, ed. U. Beier and B. Gbadamosi. **Paul's Book Arcade:** 'Lullaby' from *Poetry of the Maori* by B. Mitcalfe, 1961. **Penguin Books Ltd:** 'The Mother's Song to a Baby' tr. Peter Freuchen, from *Voices*, vol. 3, ed. Geoffrey Summerfield, 1968; 'The Washing of the Infant' by Su Shih, from *The Penguin Book of Chinese Verse*, tr. Robert Kotewall and Norman L. Smith, ed. A. R. Davis, 1962. **Penguin USA:** 'On the First Night' from *Ordinary Miracles* by Erica Jong, 1983. **Poetry Publications:** 'A Poem for My Son' by Bibhu Padhi, from *The Golden Voices: Poets from Orissa Writing in English*, ed. Niranjan Mohanty, 1986. **Unicorn Press:** 'Baby Where Has Your Father Gone?' by Momoro Kini, from *Words of Paradise: Poetry of Papua New Guinea*, ed. Ulli Beier, 1973. **Virago Press:** 'To Our Daughter' by Jennifer Armitage from *Women's Poetry of the 19th and 20th Centuries*, 1982.

The Publishers have made every effort to contact holders of copyright material. If you have not received our correspondence, please contact us for inclusion in future editions.

Sources for 'Birthing Traditions'

Para. 1: 'Folk-lore, Medical Superstitions – The Ash Tree' by William John Thomas, from *Peasant Customs and Savage Myths: Selections from the British Folklorists*, ed. Richard M. Dorson, Routledge & Kegan Paul, 1968. **Para. 2:** *Growing Up in Shona Society: From Birth to Marriage* by Michael Gelfand, Mambo Press, 1979. **Paras. 3-4:** 'The Great Team: Theses and Viewpoints' by George Laurence Gomme, from *Peasant Customs and Savage Myths*. **Paras. 5 & 13:** *Aboriginal Siberia* by M. A. Czaplicka, Clarendon Press, 1914. **Para. 6:** *Everyday Life in the Muslim Middle East*, ed. Donna Lee Bowen and Evelyn A. Early, Indiana University Press, 1993. **Para. 7:** *Rural Malay Women in Tradition and Transition* by Heather Strange, Praeger Publishers, 1981. **Para. 8:** *African Birth: Childbirth in Cultural Transition* by Beverley Chalmers Berev, River Club, 1990. **Para. 9:** 'Basic Themes in Akha Culture' by Paul W. Lewis, from *Contributions to Southeast Asian Ethnography*, No. 1, September 1982, 'Studies of Ethnic Minority Peoples'. **Para. 10:** 'Passing through Trees, Stones' by Ambrose Merton, from *Peasant Customs and Savage Myths*. **Para. 11:** 'Some Aspects of Pon' by Chogyam Trungpa, from *Himalayan Anthropology: The Indo-Tibetan Interface*, ed. James F. Fisher, Mouton Publishers, 1978. **Para. 12:** *The Hill of Flutes: Life, Love and Poetry in Tribal India – A Portrait of the Santals* by W. G. Archer, George Allen & Unwin, 1974. **Paras. 14 & 16-17:** *Mamatoto: A Celebration of Birth*, ed. Barbara Aria and the Body Shop Team, Virago Press, 1991. **Para. 15:** *An Anthology of Chuvash Poetry*, tr. Peter France, ed. Gennady Aygi, Forest Books, 1991. **Para. 18:** *Ancient Futures: Learning from Ladakh* by Helena Norberg-Hodge, Rider Books, 1991.

Barefoot Books
124 Walcot Street
Bath BA1 5BG

Copyright © 1996 by Nikki Siegen-Smith

First published in Great Britain in 1996 by Barefoot Books Ltd
This edition published in 2005
This book was typeset in New Caledonia
The illustrations were reproduced from a selection of prints and slides

Graphic design by DW Design, London
Colour separation by Grafiscan, Verona
Printed and bound in Hong Kong by South China Printing Co. Ltd

This book has been printed on 100% acid-free paper

ISBN 1-84148-492-X

British Cataloguing-in-Publication Data: a catalogue record for this book is available from the British Library

1 3 5 7 9 8 6 4 2